RECHARGE YOUR TEAM:
Keep Them
Going and Going...

Donna Deeprose

AMA Management Briefing

AMA Publications Division
American Management Association

For information on how to order additional copies of this publication, see page 74.

Library of Congress Cataloging-in-Publication Data

Deeprose, Donna.
    Recharge your team: keep them going and going — / Donna
Deeprose.
        p. cm.
    ISBN 0-8144-2366-3
    1. Teams in the workplace. 2. Employee motivation. I. Title.
    HD66.D434   1998
    658.3'14—dc21   98-8850
                                                  CIP

This Management Briefing has been distributed to all members enrolled in the American Management Association International.

First printing

Contents

Acknowledgments

This Management Briefing exists because many busy people carved time from their hectic schedules to talk openly to me about the problems teams wrestled with in their organizations and the solutions they had discovered. I want to thank them all (listed here alphabetically by company name): Mil Rosseau of Autonoon in Belgium; Christine Burbank and Jane DeLong of Blue Cross Blue Shield of Montana; Marc Bridgham of Boeing; Kristen Machen and John Fair of Chevron Petroleum Technology Company; Sherri Lindenberg of The Equitable; Steve Nielsen and Alec McCommon of Federal Express; John Kordsmeier and Jean Maier of Northwestern Mutual Life; Sean Stevens, who works with a Fortune 500 health products company; Kevin Haurin of Picker International; Duncan Crundwell of Solid State Logic Organ Systems; and Michael Bailey of TACOM-TARDEC.

Thanks, also, to Kathy Belcher of the Center for the Study of Work Teams at the University of North Texas and Peter Sorensen of Ginkgo Enterprises, a Dallas consulting firm, who connected me to many of the people above.

Introduction

A New York manager in a newly merged conglomerate participated enthusiastically in a cross-functional team whose purpose was to coordinate the work of people producing products for the same market. The team took on the challenge with vigor and nine months after its inauguration brought forth its first accomplishment, a catalog that incorporated all products for the market. Flushed with victory but a little worn out and confronting formidable backlogs on their regular jobs, the team members backed off when the leader tried to pull them together to identify and tackle their next task. In fact, as the manager put it, "It looked like the team had just fizzled out."

A manufacturing plant in the Southwest started out as an experiment in self-directed work teams and soon became a model of a team-based operation. But with its parent corporation as a captive customer, the plant was under little pressure to attend to its bottom-line financial results. Then, after a corporate merger, the parent cracked down hard.

"Get fixed or we'll close the door," is how one spokesperson remembers the parent's warning. To ensure that the plant got fixed, the parent sent in new management that instituted sweeping controls.

What happened to the teams? The new management insists they have not been abandoned. But to those who were there during the plant's heyday, it looks like teams were thrown out the window.

"Just now," says the spokesperson, "we're redefining what we really want in place in terms of teams."

The Perils of Teams

Business is avidly embracing all kinds of teams as the fading century relaxes its grip on its ideals of scientific management and rugged individualism. But

1

what both the New York conglomerate and the Southwestern manufacturing plant discovered is that business teams, however robust they appear, are still delicate organisms, at risk of succumbing to any number of internal and external threats. And sometimes, just when a team—or a plant full of teams—seems strongest, unanticipated problems can arise that range from time stealing and energy sapping to life threatening.

You might call it the sophomore slump, although it usually occurs during the team's second spurt rather than precisely in its second year. It occurs when the start up phase is over, the battle to organize has been won, the struggle for organizational recognition has been achieved, and—seemingly—the dream of a cohesive unit has been realized. Perhaps there is a slight slackening of vigilance that the team had had to maintain just to stay alive long enough to spread its wings and begin to fly. Or, perhaps, it's just that having overcome the first hurdles, there's a new batch waiting around the bend.

This book is about that new batch of problems along with solutions that have worked for companies in the United States and Europe. Some maladies—like burnout and turnover—probably infect a team for the first time as it reaches a degree of maturity. Others—such as erratic organizational support and tensions among team members—are undoubtedly issues the team struggled with in its embryonic stage; now they return with a vengeance.

The Many Faces of Teams

Workplace teams take many forms, address many purposes, and have many different names, but they fall into two general categories. First, there are the teams variously known as cross-functional teams, product improvement teams, process improvement teams, and program teams. These may be short- or long-lived or even permanent. What these teams have in common is that they combine people from a variety of functions who work together toward a joint goal. To simplify terminology, this book refers to all of these as *project teams*.

A second broad category of business teams has upended the basic structure of countless manufacturing and service organizations over the last decade. These are work unit teams that assume most of the responsibilities formerly reserved for the unit's supervisor. Such a unit may be called an autonomous work team, a self-managed team, or a self-directed team. It is a small group of employees who share responsibilities for a block of work; the team plans, schedules, and assigns work and makes decisions related to production and personnel. This book uses the name *self-directed work team (SDWT)* for all teams of this type.

How the Book Is Organized

There are 10 chapters in this book.

Each of the first nine chapters focuses on one broad problem, which is really a generalization of a number of more specific problems, which are observable manifestations of the broader one. Chapter 1, for example, looks at several things team members do when they have conflicting priorities. For instance, project team members may start skipping meetings because they are too busy with other tasks. Or they may come to the meetings but use them to resolve other issues. SDWT members may struggle to keep up with team tasks as functional work piles up. The chapter also deals with what happens when the team itself loses sight of changing priorities and gets stuck on a treadmill of activities that no longer reflect organizational needs.

Chapters 1 through 9 each include charts that provide an at-a-glance reference: problems, possible causes, actions to try that have worked for other organizations (often presented in descending order of choice, the last action in a category being in the nature of "if all else fails"), and ways to prevent the problem from happening again. The narrative part of the chapter adds detail and company examples to the description of the problem and suggested solutions.

As much as possible, the book focuses on solutions that the team itself, or the team leader, can apply to each problem. But there are situations— some of them caused by management—where only management can get the team back on track. In these cases the book recommends actions for management to take.

Prevention Is the Best Cure

The original purpose of this book was to compile solutions to common problems. But a recurring phrase wove through the responses of interviewees who shared their experience and expertise: "That shouldn't happen if . . . ." No reader struggling with a problem now would be gratified to discover here only what the team or the manager *should have done.* Nevertheless, it would

be shortsighted to ignore all the advice for keeping these problems from happening in the first place—or happening again.

In fact, there are a few vaccines that protect against many team ail-
ments, as a glance at all the charts will show. So rather than repeat these from
chapter to chapter, Chapter 10, the final chapter in the book, is devoted to
preventing problems. It includes a sample document a team lives by, a document that can be especially effective when it is written or updated after a
team has struggled through real life, identified the obstacles, and sharpened
its techniques for overcoming them.

Chapter 1

Conflicting Priorities

It will happen. Everywhere in business today, people are wearing many hats, assuming ever-increasing responsibilities. So in the life of any permanent or long-lived team, there will be times when progress will falter because members are juggling too many balls. The manager of a project team member may call on the person to redouble efforts on a high priority task back in the work unit. In a self-directed work team, a big new order, growing backlog, or unexpected customer demand may draw workers' attention away from their concentration on learning and assuming increased supervisory responsibilities.

Burdened by conflicting priorities, team members may respond in ways that shortchange team tasks and bypass team processes. They may skip team meetings, asserting they are "too busy"; they may attend the meetings but use the time to talk about different issues they share with other members of the team; they may fall behind on promised deliverables. The sooner the team leader intervenes, the less likelihood that a few isolated instances will grow into patterns that erode the team's viability.

Confirm the Root of the Problem

When situations like these start to occur, the team leader's first task is to confirm that "other priorities" isn't a polite euphemism for burnout or loss of interest in the team's purpose and activities. Those are different problems, covered in later chapters, and while the symptoms may be similar, some of the solutions are quite different. But connecting with team members outside the formal meetings is a good starting point whatever the underlying cause of members' withdrawal.

Jean Maier, vice president of life benefits at Northwestern Mutual Life in Milwaukee, whose work with project teams has dealt with issues ranging from revising claims forms to reorganizing a work area, sets up luncheons with team members throughout the year to keep in contact, shore up interest, and uncover problems. One problem that may surface is that the member's manager doesn't see the team's work as a high priority activity.

Negotiate with the Manager

When it's a team member's manager who puts a low priority on a project team's work, the first person to approach that manager should be the team member who reports to her. John Kordsmeier, director of organization development at Northwestern Mutual, says that discussion should strive for:

- A fresh look at the team's purpose and its need for the member's skills and expertise.

- A reassessment of the priority placed on the team's work by the organization and the manager.

- A commitment by the manager either to make the team member available to the team for a specified percentage of the person's time or to assign another employee, with the necessary knowledge and skills, to the team to replace the original member.

There's nothing wrong with ratchetting up the pressure a notch when team members can't get support from their managers for projects the organization has rated as high priorities. The next step is up to the team leader. "If I don't think a member is getting his manager's support, I'll talk to the manager," Maier says.

Or this may be the time to enlist the assistance of the team's sponsor. A sponsor, Maier explains, is someone, outside the team, who gives authority to the team and breaks down barriers that may arise. Often the sponsor comes from upper management but not always. At Northwestern Mutual, team sponsors may be anyone from a manager all the way up to the CEO, Kordsmeier says. A committed sponsor may be able to convince a manager of the team's importance when the member or team leader can't.

At Federal Express in Memphis, Alec McCommon, FedEx Leadership Institute advisor, knows from personal experience what it's like when you are the team leader and many of the members get pulled away to attend to other priorities. That happened to McCommon several years ago when he headed up a project team to study "anything that looked like a self-directed team" at FedEx prior to the company's full-scale launch into a team-based environment. The result, he recalls, is that most of the job ended up on his plate. He remembers, as if it were yesterday, compiling the responses and analyzing the data of a 21-question survey that brought in seven piles of factor-related questions.

Steve Nielsen, the Institute director, places much of the responsibility for what happened to McCommon on management—both himself and managers of the team members. "The team members were not getting support from their hierarchy," he recalls. "The project was a priority to us but not for them. If I had done a good job of communicating that priority to others, maybe the team members they provided would have stuck it out."

He adds, "I could have told them, 'Here's how we can make this better,' or better yet, I could have asked people, 'What can we do to make this better, make it a priority for your time?'"

Change the Process to Meet Team Members' Needs

The key to solving priority problems isn't always outside the team. Sometimes a team can find ways to be less of a drain on its members' time and energy.

With hindsight, McCommon believes he could have set up a system that would have demanded less of everyone—including himself. "If I had to do it again, I'd make sure we had a format and process that would have allowed people to dovetail their efforts more smoothly into a final product."

To illustrate the difficulties the team had, he adds, "We had both Macs and PCs. We didn't even have a standard font."

Sometimes the team leader needs to cast a critical eye on the way the team is operating to see if it's driving members away to seemingly more important tasks. Maier of Northwestern Mutual Life recommends:

■ Rotate membership. "People shouldn't have to be assigned to a project forever," she remarks.

- Ask yourself, "Does this team really have to meet?" If there's another way to accomplish the objective, do that instead.

- If a meeting can't be avoided, choose a time of day and location that are most convenient for everyone.

- Keep the agenda crisp. If some members' expertise isn't needed for awhile, don't include them in meetings. Send them minutes instead.

- Schedule a lot of meetings very quickly, rather than stretch them out over a long period of time. Or arrange a half-day marathon to resolve an issue in one fell swoop.

- Keep the team focused.

To Maier's last point, Sherri Lindenberg of Equitable Life in New York, would say "Amen." Now vice president of Equitable's Strategic Planning Unit, Lindenberg has spent the better part of her career in jobs with little or no staff, always having to put together teams from individuals across the organization to get things done. These days at Equitable almost everyone is on at least one project team—sometimes several—in additional to his or her regular position.

The result is that team membership overlaps a lot, with several people sharing membership in more than one team. One outgrowth is a tendency for people to take care of Team A's business at Team B's meetings. Lindenberg had to fight this in a team charged with crafting a new vision document.

Members came to New York from all over the country to work on the document from 8 a.m. to 4 p.m. But, during the same visit, many of them were also attending meeting of teams to address other issues like restructuring field offices and improving financial planning tools. When those issues flowed into the vision document meeting discussion, Lindenberg knew she had to draw the line. It took a few tries, but she finally got the team to agree to stick to the agenda.

"I was concerned," she admits, "because there were people senior to me. I didn't want them to perceive me as stepping out of line. So I went to these people after and solicited their help to make sure we were able to stay on the agenda next time."

Monitor Your Own Time

Most basic perhaps is each team member's responsibility to monitor her own ability to keep up with everything she commits to. "I'm in a new job,"

Lindenberg says, "but I didn't want to give up some of the teams I've been working on. Then I realized that I can't give them the time they deserve anymore, so I have to find someone to replace me. My former job was mostly team-based activities and I'm finding replacements for myself on those teams."

Priority changes for individuals aren't always the result of time crunches. As Kordsmeier points out, one of the reasons people choose to join teams is to learn something new. Individuals who have served on a team for a long time may feel the team no longer offers them a chance to develop new skills. For them, that reduces team efforts to a pretty low priority. To illustrate his point, he uses a hypothetical example of a long-term member of a standing team at Northwestern Mutual that addresses disability income insurance. If that person decides he has learned everything he needs to know about DI, Kordsmeier explains, then it is time for him to leave and give someone else the same opportunity.

Priority Clashes in SDWTs

When priorities clash in self-directed work teams, it's usually between functional tasks and the associates' newer team or administrative duties. When it boils down to a choice between serving the customer or attending a team meeting—or, even less desirable, doing paperwork that professional administrators used to do—it's easy to say, "No contest! The customer comes first." And yet that paperwork needs to get done, too, or a lot of critical company processes slow down. And those meetings are crucial for teams to develop into well-oiled units that expertly manage their own businesses.

As SDWTs mature, they find ways to balance both needs.

Cover for Each Other

Picker International, headquartered in Cleveland, a medical diagnostic imaging field service organization, has 54 SDWTs, which it calls "customer focus teams." Groups of field service engineers within a specified geographic territory, customer focus teams are charged with satisfying customer requirements faster and better than ever before. In a critical health care field, that means responding to customer calls instantly.

For Kevin Haurin, manager of Quality Driven Leadership Initiatives, the challenge is facilitating team meetings with beepers going off all the time in the room. No one questions the engineers' priorities when they leave meetings to take customer calls or even to go to the customer's location. But it plays havoc with the team process.

It's a problem the most mature teams are beginning to solve. Not long ago at a meeting, Haurin was delighted with how a team handled the situation when a call came in from a customer whose assigned engineer was deeply involved in a complex discussion. Instead of disrupting the meeting while the engineer handled the customer problem, another engineer—less involved in the meeting task—jumped up and took the call, handled the customer problem over the phone, and came back.

For one engineer to back up another that way is no easy accomplishment at Picker. For one thing, until recently each engineer concentrated on one product line. When the engineers formed teams, they learned multiple product lines—what Picker calls modalities: x-ray, nuclear, computed tomography, magnetic resonance imaging, etc. Added to that is the fact that service is a very relationship-oriented business. Customers with problems with million-dollar medical diagnostic equipment don't want just any engineer, they want *their* engineer, the one they trust who they know will do the job right. So to expand the engineer/customer relationship to a team/customer relationship, the team created lists of customer characteristics, including human factors like whom you need to talk to, how to talk to them, whom to check off with before you leave.

What the team discovered is that when the customer is always first priority, it helps for every team member to know every customer.

At Blue Cross Blue Shield of Montana in Helena, the billing service team sometimes faces a similar problem. When inventory gets to the point where it's overwhelming, says Team Coach Christine Burbank, it's easy for team members to get away from the team concept and plead, "Just leave us alone to do our job."

When that happens, the team holds a team meeting to refocus, redefine the issue as a team problem, and look for team solutions. "They forget," Burbank says, "that the rest of the team can help. And other teams can help, too."

Up the Ante on the Less Favored Work

At TACOM-TARDEC, the U.S. Army Tank-Automotive Research, Development and Engineering Center in Warren, Michigan—1995 winner of the Presidential Award for Quality—members of SDWTs bemoan the time-consuming administrative work that takes them away from their customer-funded development projects. This paperwork used to be taken care of by administrative personnel before the organization, like most private industry, got leaner. Now the engineers, scientists, and technicians have to do it. They call it "ash and trash."

Michael Bailey, quality team leader, sympathizes. "The teams love being able to focus on customers," he says, "It's all this ash and trash that's bothering them."

Still, those dreary traditional business requirements—financial reports and the like—don't go away.

Besides the fact that it's tedious, the administrative work had another disincentive. It wasn't recognized in associates' performance ratings. "They were doing up to 25 percent administrative work and they weren't being rated for it," Bailey notes.

So TACOM-TARDEC built it into the rating system. Now, in performance ratings, associates get recognized for responsibilities like "answering requests from headquarters in X days in a timely fashion and quality manner." That's helped raise the priority of ash and trash.

Keep the Team's Priorities in Sync with the Organization's

Finally, teams sometimes confront a problem of conflicting priorities that's quite different from the one individual members wrestle with when they find themselves with too much to do. As a company refines its strategies and priorities, teams have to take stock to ensure their priorities still match those of the organization.

Lindenberg of Equitable stresses that "it's important that the leader makes sure the team doesn't lose sight of its overall purpose, sidetracked by short-term priorities. It might be necessary to assess changes in the marketplace or the business environment to make sure the original plan is still the right track to be on.

"We still want to put out marketing information," she adds, "but it's not our top priority."

Every team needs to be careful not to get locked into a narrow view of its purpose. Unless it keeps up to date on needs and goals of the broader organization, support for the team will wane and it will wither due to its own shortsightedness.

CONFLICTING PRIORITIES

PROBLEM: Member(s) "too busy" to attend meetings of project team or work on team tasks.

Possible Causes	Actions to Take	Ways to Prevent
Individual given additional non-team assignments by manager.	Individual and manager resolve through joint priority setting. Team coach or sponsor resolves priorities with manager. If necessary, member leaves team. Manager provides a replacement who has appropriate skills, knowledge.	Create a team contract that includes: • Signed buy-in by managers. • How much time team members are to spend on team tasks. • Steps to take to replace members if necessary.
Individual is spread too thin among several teams.	If necessary, individual finds appropriate temporary or permanent replacement for self on team.	For permanent team, set up a schedule for rotating members in and out.
Team is inefficient in its use of time.	Meet only when issue cannot be resolved in another way. Keep meetings convenient, attendance limited, and agendas tight. Block the work into a tight time frame.	Build rules for meetings into team charter. Build sunset date into charter, along with schedule for reassessing team needs.

PROBLEM: At project team meetings, members discuss projects not related to the team.

Possible Causes	Actions to Take	Ways to Prevent
Team members are also working together on other teams or ongoing programs.	Be adamant about sticking to agenda.	After meeting, team leader meets with members separately to solicit their help in keeping team on track.

PROBLEM: In self-directed work team, members shortchange team and administrative tasks to attend to critical functional job needs.

Possible Causes	Actions to Take	Ways to Prevent
No processes are in place to integrate team/administrative work with functional work.	Designate backups. Provide cross training, checklists, job aids so members can back up each other in functional work.	Team charter lists roles and responsibilities including getting cross trained and backing up teammates.
Members are rewarded primarily for functional performance.	See Chapter 8: *Growing Resentment: "I Don't Get Paid for This."*	Include measurable goals for team and administrative tasks in the performance management system.

PROBLEM: Team is spinning wheels pursuing short-term priorities that no longer match organization's needs. Organization's support for team wanes.

Possible Causes	Actions to Take	Ways to Prevent
Team failed to recognize when changes in environment made team efforts obsolete.	Review what team was supposed to accomplish, what it has accomplished, and what is left to be done. Reassess the marketplace and changing organizational goals. Determine what changes team must make in short-term priorities to meet long-term goal.	Team charter includes mission statement. Review regularly to ensure team is pursuing appropriate priorities.

Chapter 2

Loss of Focus

Y ou are in a team meeting. For the third time someone asks, "Tell me again. What is it we're supposed to be doing now?" Instead of glaring at the person for wasting the team's valuable time, the other team members look up hopefully, waiting for someone to enlighten them all.

Unless this team gets refocused fast, members won't be sitting around wondering what they are supposed to be doing anymore. They'll go their own ways. The team will fade into a blurry memory.

What causes a team to lose focus? It might be something specific, like failure to regroup and look at the broader picture after one objective has been met. Or a problem may arise that stymies the team, causing its members to question the team's purpose. Or sometimes, it's just creeping ennui that settles in when a team has been together a long time.

When Success Impedes Progress

Ironically, sometimes what causes a team to lose focus is accomplishing an objective. Remember the manager, at the beginning of the book, whose project team put out a catalog but lost sight of its broader mission: to coordinate all efforts for a single market.

"We were so successful," the manager reflects, "that mentally I think we felt our job was done."

Expert teamers suggest more than one approach to take with a team that has bogged down after completing its first task.

14

Redefine the Team Purpose

When a team can't move past its first accomplishment, there's a good chance its purpose was defined either too vaguely or too narrowly. While a catalog was something the team could focus on, the members found it harder to rally around the mission of coordinating the work of the merged units. In fact, just the opposite occurred, and conflicts around territorialism surfaced, eroding the team even further.

Even when a team's purpose was originally clearly defined, asserts Jane DeLong, vice president of Corporate Resources and Quality Management at Blue Cross Blue Shield of Montana, it's crucial to revisit it at least annually.

Whether for critical rejuvenation or annual maintenance, DeLong recommends that teams review their purpose, ground rules, boundaries, tasks, measures of success, role and responsiblities, and meeting rules.

"It comes back to: Do we understand the goal? What is the end result, and how will we know when we reach it?" concurs Steve Nielsen of Federal Express. He adds, "The team needs to measure its progress along the way. Constantly showing measurable impact gives momentum."

Determine What Comes Next

One approach to reinvigorate a team that has met its first objective, recommends Mil Rosseau of Autonoom in Waasmunster, Belgium, is to involve the team in the followup to their first accomplishment. To illustrate, he tells the story of a team he worked with at Sabena Airline. It was a Care Team, devoted to "taking care of passengers in trouble."

"In Europe," Rosseau explains, "we have big problems with flight delays because of Customs and legal checks. Passengers get lost in administration between flights."

He describes the team's progress: "After a year, the team came up with a number of solutions that were quick, easy, and available on the computer network—things like reissuing tickets, rerouting, arranging lodging. The regular agents could now take these over.

Rosseau had learned from experience with teams in other companies that when a team's work gets integrated into the everyday life of the company, "the team is like a mother who has to give her baby up for adoption—she doesn't want to do it."

So Rosseau guided the Care Team into defining followup tasks: training the regular agents in using the new tools and checking to see if the solutions were being regularly applied.

"The team also gave itself a new goal: benchmarking customer service at airports all over the world."

Decide: Should a New Team Take Over?

Some companies favor an alternative approach to following up on a team's accomplishment. DeLong describes what Blue Cross Blue Shield of Montana has done with changemaker teams to develop new systems:

"Many of our changemaker teams were functioning for a couple of years," she says. "Once the systems were developed, we celebrated with a lunch and offered our appreciation. Now we're in implementation. We changed the team membership and changed the name."

Ask Yourself: Is the Team's Job Done?

It's important to recognize when a team's job is done and celebrate the accomplishments. "Letting a team go down hill is frustrating for everyone. You need to recognize if a team is disintegrating and either add a refocusing opportunity or say thanks and disband it," advises DeLong.

Rosseau agrees, describing how a Belgian distribution company, Colruyt, ensures teams don't lose focus.

"Colruyt has teams to make improvements in the work situation," he explains. "Every time a team reaches a goal, it disbands, allowing people to stay out of teams for awhile."

"Team effort is like religion," he adds. "People will come back to it. If you force them to stay on board, they'll lose momentum."

Marc Bridgham, an internal organization development consultant at Boeing, who spends about half his time in Dallas and the other half working with Boeing teams in other locations, concurs. "Don't try to manufacture energy when it doesn't need to be there," he recommends. "Don't get all worried when you may just be taking a needed rest."

When a Problem Stumps the Team

When a team uncovers an unexpected problem outside its area of expertise, it can waste energy and get desolate before it takes a productive approach.

What it needs to do is analyze the problem, then identify and acquire the help it needs. Sometimes this is a trial and error process.

Christine Burbank of Blue Cross Blue Shield of Montana saw this happen in a team whose purpose was to increase the use of the company's voice response unit (VRU).

"What we found," recalls Burbank, "was an integrity problem, but at first we were floundering because we weren't expecting that. We hadn't heard anyone say they weren't getting the correct responses."

Uncovering the integrity problem didn't get them on the right track immediately.

"For a couple of weeks we had a tester involved, but it was not the right time for that," says Burbank.

The team was unfocused. "We'd go into meetings and look around at each other wondering what we were doing there," she remembers. "When you have a meeting in which the business is skewed, it's really frustrating. We'd come out of meetings asking, 'What in the world have we accomplished?'"

Finally the team members sat down and brainstormed, looked at facts and figures, and realized that what they were missing was input from a business analyst.

"We'd been thinking of recommending turning off the VRU," Burbank says, "and that would have been a mistake. The business analyst was able to look at the problems and say, 'Oh we can fix that.'"

A team struggling with an overwhelming problem may need to reach outside of itself for help. A skilled facilitator can keep team problem solving on track.

If the team needs expertise or skills it can't locate on its own, that's a good time to call on the sponsor to use his or her networks to find people with the necessary capabilities.

When Energy Wanes

As a team toils on over time, even when it is making progress, its achievements may not feel noteworthy enough to keep members consistently focused and revved up.

"It's not hard to get a new team energized and decide what to do," says Bridgham of Boeing. "The hard part is to maintain focus and energy through the ongoing daily slog."

LOSS OF FOCUS		
PROBLEM: Project team completes one objective, can't decide what to do next.		
Possible Causes	**Actions to Take**	**Ways to Prevent**
Team purpose was defined too narrowly or too vaguely.	Redefine team purpose. Determine long-term goal and actions needed to achieve it. Enlist sponsor's help to set direction for team. If first task was to make policy, either: • Involve the team in implementation, or • Create a new team with new members to manage implementation.	Team charter includes: • Mission • Long-term goal. • Short-term actions. • Schedule for periodic reassessment. Team charter: • Clarifies fulfillment of mission. • Includes sunset date.
The job is finished.	Say "thank you," celebrate success, and disband the team.	

Reinforce the Team's Confidence

As part of an outreach program, Bridgham worked through this kind of problem with a team of administrators, teachers, and support staff at a high school. The team had first come together a couple of years earlier to create a vision for the future. The group had all started out gung ho, Bridgham says, and a few members still were, but as a whole they had lost momentum. Instead of building a vision of the future they were stuck in past issues thathad diminished their self esteem and their own assessment of their value as educators.

To help jar them out of their discouragement, Bridgham started by helping them develop an alternative group memory, a technique he also uses with Boeing teams. The process works like this:

• *Remember the good times.* First, he has people begin by individually remembering when the organization was operating at its best. Then he asks them to share their stories in pairs. Then each pair joins another pair, each foursome joins another foursome, until finally the entire group has rejoined.

• *Share the best stories.* In the large group, he asks them to share whatever stories they want to repeat again. Just the telling, he says, begins to change things.

PROBLEM: Team is stymied by unanticipated problems.

Possible Causes	Actions to Take	Ways to Prevent
First analysis of issue failed to raise underlying problem or situation has changed since team began.	Bring in a facilitator to help define the problem and determine next steps through team problem solving.	Train team in problem solving.
	Enlist outside experts to guide team in solving the problem.	
	Enlist help of sponsor to identify people in or outside the organization with the necessary skills.	

PROBLEM: Project team is fizzling out, enthusiasm waning.

Possible Causes	Actions to Take	Ways to Prevent
Team has toiled on too long without notable achievements	Build a team activity around memories of past achievements to reinforce team's confidence and self-esteem.	Develop and regularly use vehicles for assessment: • Instrument to rate meeting effectiveness used after every meeting. • Team effectiveness analysis: What do we do well? What do we need to change?
		Celebrate small victories.
		Regularly reassess mission, long and short term goals, actions to achieve them.

- *Distill the common ingredients.* The next step is to analyze the stories and identify the common ingredients: what made each a positive experience. In the school team, some of their stories were bittersweet: They remembered how they had all pulled together one year when several students had committed suicide. And they recalled how the students had joined together to confront the unwanted media attention the suicides had elicited. Remembering how united they had been, they got quite emotional, Bridgham recalls.

- *Build a vision for now,* based on what was powerful in their real past experience. For the school team, togetherness was at the core of its new vision. Its first action step was to create a physical space in the school where people could just hang out together.

To refocus and rejuvenate a team like the one at the high school, the process Bridgham uses may take two days offsite. "But," he says, "if you do it as maintenance, it's five minutes every month or so."

Sherri Lindenberg at Equitable Life concurs that shining up the past is key to jumpstarting the future for a team that's lost its drive. "Most of what we're doing is not huge wins," she notes, "so it's easy to look back and wonder what we've been doing here. Sometimes, when we look back, our accomplishments look less significant than they were."

So she looks for ways to celebrate small milestones. Sometimes she gives small gifts. Once she gave all the members of a team she led 10-minute phone cards that an outside vendor had left with her. "The card itself didn't mean that much, but it called attention to their participation and showed I valued it."

Assess On-going Performance

Marc Bridgham uses another device to keep teams on track: regular use of team assessment instruments. There are several good ones available commercially, but Bridgham says it's more powerful for the team to create its own, deciding what's most important to it. He recalls one management team that hated meetings. So the members created an instrument to assess their meeting behavior and rated themselves with it at the end of every meeting. Just going through it every time helped them sharpen up their meetings and make them more bearable.

But, he adds, the simplest mechanism is just to ask yourselves regularly: What's working well? What do we want to do differently? He advises:

- *Concentrate on the positive.* It's more important to sustain what's working than to get tied up in knots about what isn't.

- *Phrase problems as requests:* "These are the things I'd like us to do differently."

- *Negotiate through the requests.*

Don't wait for something to go drastically wrong before using this mechanism, Bridgham warns. Do it once a month as maintenance." Over time, he asserts, the team will get better and better, creating more and more energy.

Chapter 3

Lack of Cooperation, Communication With Other Teams

"**W**e tore down the functional silos. But man is a wall-builder, and we left the materials lying around so teams picked up the materials and built new walls around themselves."

John Fair at Chevron was explaining the need to foster more cooperative behavior among teams.

Self-directed work teams were supposed to break down the barriers that in hierarchical organizations block the sharing of knowledge and skills throughout the organization. But a variety of factors combine to encourage insular behavior in teams: reward systems that offer no incentives for helping other teams, team-building activities that concentrate exclusively on building intra-team relationships, and the sense of security and belonging that a tight little group provides.

"We were trying to push [intra]team behaviors first," says Fair. "There were no drivers in place to promote teams working together."

Among organizations with adolescent SDWTs, stories abound of teams so caught up in their own visions that they forgot the larger one of the whole company. There's the one about two teams, each building a different piece of the same final product, that unveiled their components only to discover they didn't fit together. There are numerous episodes of teams so focused on their own tasks that they flatly refused to assist another team in more need. And there are cautionary tales of teams that set out to steal each other's business with cutthroat tactics.

Breaking Down the Silos

Kristin Machen is a member of Chevron's Produced Fluids Separation and Treatment Team. One of its responsibilities is to develop cost effective ways to treat the water pumped out of the ground with oil so the water can be disposed of in an environmentally safe way.

"My team works with facilities that handle produced water," she explains. "Others with reservoirs that are the source of the water, and another with water chemistry. It would make sense if all of these worked together."

Overlap team memberships. Chevron is trying different ways to make that happen. One way is the formation of multidisciplinary teams. Some of Machen's teammates spend 20 percent of their time on a multidisciplinary team looking at water management in general.

Chevron has also started anchoring teams that need to work together by having certain people be core members of each team. They attend all core meetings of each team and are responsible for relaying information between the two. According to Fair, that required a policy change. When Chevron Petroleum Technology first implemented teams, team members were limited to being core members of only one team. That seemed to make sense, preventing people from being spread too thin, but it cut off communication and best practice sharing. (Chevron teams can also have non-core members, whose attachment to the team is more flexible. Non-core members could always serve on more than one team but they don't attend all meetings and may not know everything a team is doing.)

Finding Resources Outside the Team

One effect of silo building is that teams and members lose their links to resources in other parts of the organization. In hierarchical systems, you might have to take a request up the ladder and wait for it to go down another ladder, back up again, and then down to you—but eventually the system worked. More likely, you knew the informal route to take to get directly to what you wanted. Sometimes, as teams get strong and insular, both the formal and the informal networks are lost.

Create a team leaders' forum. Whether you don't get what you need from another team or you are trying to serve three other teams and can't get it all done, it can be a tough environment out there, acknowledges Marc Bridghan of Boeing. What works best, he says, is for a group of team leaders to create their own forum—whether it's every Friday afternoon or every Thursday for breakfast—where they can go down a list of each other's needs and come to hand-shake agreements. It's a good way to identify and iron out potential problems, but, he warns, you've got to guard against letting the meetings degenerate into trivia.

Publish a list. At Picker International, the most forward thinking teams addressed this problem themselves, says Kevin Haurin. They compiled and shared with other teams a list of people on all teams within the geographical area who could support other teams.

Enlist the coaches. After SDWTs had been in effect at TACOM-TARDEC for a couple of years, the organization accepted the recommendation of a cross-functional "tiger team" and strengthened the role of associate directors—managers-turned-coaches. Among their new responsibilities is building linkages among teams that need to share resources.

Serve internal customers. If every team were to think of the rest of the organization as its customers, a whole new approach to resource sharing would result. Steve Nielsen of FedEx advises every team to identify its internal customers and ask each one three questions: "What do you need? What do you do with it when you get it? Are there any gaps between what you need and what you are getting?" He had to do this with five internal customers when he became director of the FedEx Leadership Institute in 1990. Every director and officer in the company had to do it, he recalls. What works for executives works equally well for teams.

Making the Pieces Fit

Marc Bridgham of Boeing describes what can happen when several different teams are working on pieces of a final product. "Essentially the progression goes like this: We take a product and divide it into components. These are the pieces; here are the teams. Go forth and do.

"Theoretically there is a comprehensive plan at the organization level and each team's plan flows from that. But what sounded good on paper gets messy in real life. Everyone can get focused on his own piece. Pretty soon, everybody comes up out of the dust and realizes, 'Whoa, we're banging up against each other.'"

One solution Boeing has tried is *integration teams.* Integration teams take different forms. Some are made up of the leaders of all the teams whose work must be integrated. Others are separate teams; sometimes being an integration team member is a full-time job. Whatever their composition, they can serve a number of roles:

> ***Proactive**—looking out for potential conflicts of authority or decisions.* For example, if different components have to be hooked up, the integration team makes sure there is agreement on how the two pieces will come together. If a system, such as electrical power, is to cross several components, the integration team determines which drives the design. And it pays attention to schedules, ensuring the parts are ready to come together at the same time.

> ***Reactive**—arbitrating* when teams can't resolve a situation among themselves.

> ***Distributing requirements.*** If a customer wants to change something, the integration team distributes the new requirements among the teams.

Overall, Bridgham sums up, "The integration team is a caretaker, watching out for the whole community, making sure everyone is in sync in terms of timing and resources."

When a Team Just Says No

In a blatant display of failure to cooperate, one team asks another for help and gets a flat "No" in reply. When teams are measured on customer satisfaction or production metrics—and most teams are—they can get very inward focused. Somebody's got to keep reminding them that meeting their own objectives is hollow unless the organization is meeting its overall goals.

"Teams can get to the point where members are saying, 'Hey, we're great,'" warns Haurin of Picker International. "Then if a team that needs help—say, a member is sick—goes to the 'great' team and says, 'Will you send us an engineer?' the answer may be no because the risk is too great. The healthy team may be thinking, 'If we send you an engineer we may not be able to satisfy our customers.'"

It's up to the coaches, Haurin says, to instill a different mentality in the team. Under the old hierarchies, he points out, managers learned very quickly that they needed a quid pro quo mentality: I'll support you now because, if I need something later, you may be able to help me. Teams may not have discovered that yet. So the coach needs to come in and say, "Here's how the real world works."

At the same time, he adds, they should coach the team in risk analysis so they don't put themselves too much at risk.

As a team coach, Burbank of Blue Cross Blue Shield of Montana knows how important it is to guard against insular thinking. She recalls a situation when "one team's inventory went way high. We were a little behind, but the other team was way behind."

Were they tempted to focus on their own inventory problem? Sure. The company has an incentive system based on company-wide goals, but teams have to meet their own goals to participate in it. Nevertheless, the team refocused its attention on the broader need and pitched in to reduce the other team's backlog.

Besides the realization that if teams don't help each other the overall company goals might not be met, there was an even bigger motivator. "What we've done is refocus on our customer," Burbank says. "When one team gets way behind, we're hurting our customers."

The organization publishes a weekly inventory report, and the coaches discuss it when they meet each week. But, Burbank stresses, it is not just the coaches who drive the need to help across teams. "The team members sell the need to help others too," she asserts.

Escalating to Competition

Not cooperating is bad enough, but it's not the worst that can happen.

"The worst I've heard," says Fair of Chevron, where teams get their funding from their customers, "was a team going out and saying to another team's customer, 'You know that team you've always dealt with—don't fund them. We've got better technology." Customers can provoke competition between teams, he notes, by shopping around to find that team that will do the job for less, getting the teams bidding against each other.

LACK OF COOPERATION, COMMUNICATION WITH OTHER TEAMS

PROBLEM: Team cannot get help or resources it needs from other parts of the organization.

Possible Causes	Actions to Take	Ways to Prevent
Self-directed work teams have built walls around themselves, paralleling the "silos" in traditional functional organizations.	Develop and publish a list of people throughout the organization who can provide the necessary services. Expand it by sharing it with other teams. Make some people members of more than one team. Give coaches or sponsors the responsibility to locate resources.	Include specific responsiblities for supporting other teams in original team assignments. Build these responsiblities into team charters.

PROBLEM: Final product is harmed because input from two or more teams doesn't mesh.

Possible Causes	Actions to Take	Ways to Prevent
Teams working at cross purposes, overlapping and/or ignoring the work of other, related teams.	Create integration teams to identify and resolve potential conflicts in processes and outputs, determine who drives the final outcome, and ensure that schedules match.	Schedule periodic reassessments of responsibilities toward and relationships with other teams, especially those working on related projects.

This is a problem management needs to address. In response to strong-arm marketing tactics by one team member, Fair has spoken with the product and service line manager to get his commitment to coach the employee on his behavior and support teams working together. Over the longer run, he expects an organizational change to have an impact. Instead of teams reporting to only one product service line manager, the company has started to assign more than one product service line manager per team. Since each manager has several teams, that increases the size of each overlapping family. Rivalry, Fair says, is usually among teams reporting to different managers. This will erase those boundaries.

PROBLEM: Team refuses to help another Team.

Possible Causes	Actions to Take	Ways to Prevent
Team's own workload is high.	Coach team in quid pro quo mentality: I'll support you because someday you may be able to help me. Provide recognition for helping outside team. Make it a status symbol. Focus on shared goal: meeting customer needs. Coach team in feedback and joint-problem solving techniques they can use in communicating with other teams. Joint problem solving by team leaders or coaches.	Team Charter defines situations in which team will put work of other before its own. Build cooperative behaviors into performance assessment. Base a part of incentive compensation on success of larger group.

PROBLEM: Teams aggressively compete with each other, going after each other's projects.

Possible Causes	Actions to Take	Ways to Prevent
Reward system encourages rivalry.	Educate teams on the link between the performance of the entire organization and their own rewards. Develop criteria for working behavior that clearly distinguishes between appropriate competitive behavior, i.e., working to make your project the best, and inappropriate behavior, i.e., undermining the work of another team. If necessary, enforce the ban on inappropriate competition with punishments determined at management level.	Measure team performance against goals and standards for each team, rather than by ranking teams against each other.

Building Inter-Team Trust

Here's a recipe for superior results—or for disaster: Take two teams of highly skilled members from different disciplines and tell them they have to work hand in hand.

Without some intensive inter-team team building, you should expect fireworks. Sean Stevens, organization development specialist in a Fortune 500 health product company, was preparing to combine a health team and a safety team for project work, such as working on blood-born pathogens. Their roles are interrelated, he said, but they don't work well together. Still, the most effective methodology for the company would be to combine a medical expert and a safety expert in tandem.

Confronted with situations of this nature, Stevens brings the teams together in team-building sessions that can last two or three days. He covers such topics as overall objectives, interdependence, norms for working together, and a perception exchange—how each team sees the other. That's the opening, he says, to some deep-seated assumptions about each other that have to be addressed before rivalries disappear and people trust each other enough to work effectively together across teams.

Chapter 4

Threatened by Naysayers

"**N**ah, it'll never work." That's the clarion call of the critics, ringing out predictably to dampen enthusiasm for the team's most innovative ideas. Or, in some SDWT-based workplaces, it's a steady but unsettling muttering in the background from die-hard individualists, always on the lookout for a chance to subvert the teaming process.

Whether the naysayers are looking in from the outside or doing their damage from within a team, containing the negativism they spread can drain a lot of team resources and energy.

Don't Coddle Resisters in SDWTs

It's not unusual for a new self-directed work team to house a few stalwarts who didn't ask to be on a team, don't want to be on a team, and don't intend to have any part of this team business. Some of them come around as the team builds momentum, and some fall by the wayside. But if they are still naysaying, in overt or covert fashion, after the team has settled in, that's a problem. At best, they are a dead weight the team drags around. At worst, they seriously undermine the team's progress.

If the other members of the team can't bring them around, then it's management's responsibility to deal with them.

Team Coach Christine Burbank of Blue Cross Blue Shield of Montana explains the approach she took with employees who, given every opportunity, continued to be negative about teams. "I couldn't just let them sit apart and be naysayers," she explains. "I had to pull them aside and say 'This is the direction of the company. If you can't buy into it, you need to think about your career choices.' We had people leave because they just couldn't buy into the team concept."

Don't Be Taken In

But sometimes, especially if management is still ambivalent about teaming, the non-believers are difficult to rout. Even worse, if they get control of a team they can put on a display of teamsmanship that's perfectly convincing to the rest of the organization while destroying every semblance of real team-work from within.

John Fair, a Center of Excellence manager for Chevron Petroleum Company in La Habra, California, warns, "We hire very bright people. You can tell those skeptical about teamwork that team behavior is going to be rewarded and they are quite capable of displaying team behavior in your meetings with them even if that's not their normal behavior."

Chevron Petroleum Technology has a unique matrix structure. Center of Excellence managers have the responsibility to guide the development of long-term programs and to staff the teams that work on short- and long-term programs and day-to-day service. Product and service line managers are responsible for developing short-term and for managing work execution by the teams. Fair, who was one of Chevron's team pioneers, was off on another assignment when a team he had started struggled through several team leaders who did not buy into the self-managed team concept, behaving like the supervisors they had once been.

Support the True Believers

Coaching by e-mail, Fair helped bolster the resolve of three diehard team enthusiasts. As long as they maintained their resolve, the team had a chance. In a team of 8-12 people, he says, as few as three can hold a team together and bring others into the fold. He provided what a team in this threatened position needs:

- Business information they weren't getting elsewhere.

- A sounding board to hear their issues and help them look at the problem from all sides.

■ A shoulder—albeit a virtual one—to lean on in trying times.

The team held out. Says one of the three members who helped keep the team spirit alive, "I am not saying that there have not been a lot of ups and downs within the company and my career here, but the perks of working for this organization far outweigh any pitfalls we may have run into."

Focus on Behavior, Not Labels

What if team members agree on only one thing: They don't want to be a team? They perceive themselves as independent practitioners of different highly skilled functions, and they don't want interference from each other. Can you hold a group like this together? Is it worth trying?

Sean Stevens worked with a health and wellness team consisting of three components: medical, Employee Assistance Program, and fitness/wellness. The three formed a team but found themselves often working independently, sometimes even at odds with each other. For a person with a back ailment, the doctor might prescribe muscle relaxants while the fitness expert advised, "Don't get hooked on drugs. You need rest, stretching, and strengthening exercises."

"When I've had teams get to the point where they don't want to be a team," Stevens says, "I stress that they still need to display teamwork in those areas where they are interdependent. Team is a label. Teamwork is a behavior."

With reluctant teams like this he focuses on behaviors like:

■ Having respect for other people's skills.

■ Providing support to another team member if it doesn't meet one of your objectives.

■ Leveraging knowledge and skills among individuals on the team.

■ Being concerned for the accomplishments and goals of the whole team, sometimes even above your own personal goals.

■ Keeping others informed when it affects them.

Stevens stresses that "regardless of whether or not they have a team label, they still have to display teamwork behaviors to meet their objectives if they have a common goal and interdependencies."

Stick to Your Guns

For a project team, one of the most devastating blows comes when members offer a perfect solution to a company problem only to have it shot down by faultfinders. When the Sabena team described in Chapter 2 by Mil Rosseau took on the challenge of helping lost passengers, one of its recommendations was to purchase buses to transport people to their planes.

According to Rosseau, the initial corporate reaction was "No way."

The team could have thrown up its hands, but it didn't. Instead, it did some research, uncovering what lost passengers actually cost the company and comparing that to the cost of the buses. "It took them months," Rosseau says. "They were just agents without direct access to any of that information. But by putting out the right questions in the right way, they got the information they needed."

They also got 11 buses and chauffeurs."

Publish the Team's Accomplishments

Sean Stevens, with a health products company, says teams are particularly open to criticism if they do not gain as much return as expected in the initial time frame. Re-engineering teams are especially prone to this type of criticism. The solution, he says, is to have many small objectives—"short-term wins you plan for so that with each successive win you build more credibility in the team and in its initiative."

He recalls working with a design team on a change management project that became a target for critics who complained the team hadn't come up with anything.

"So we went back to the formal plan, bulleted everything we'd accomplished so far and published it," Stevens says, "It was actually a little bit of marketing."

Invite the Critics In

Sometimes you can win your critics over by inviting them in and asking them to be a part of what's going on," advises Marc Bridgham of Boeing.

That worked for a team that was stuck in an uphill battle with a faultfinding senior manager. When the team invited its nemesis to sit in on its meetings, the manager did a 180 degree turn.

Bridgham points out two reasons why this technique works: The naysayers get new facts and they get a chance to share their own expertise. This combination usually gets them involved.

Co-opt the Critics

When the naysayers are on the inside, objecting to a team plan because it's different from what has been done before, you've got a good chance of bringing them around if you work with them, not against them.

That's what Sherri Lindenberg of Equitable Life did with a team which put together the program for a planning meeting for the comany's local agency managers. Lindenberg thought it would be a great opportunity for computer training, badly needed for a large group of managers who were admittedly computer illiterate. A few team members adamantly resisted the idea; nothing like that had ever been done at planning meetings before.

Although she admits she didn't feel this way at the time ("All I could think was, 'Why are they doing this to me?'"), Lindenberg now says, "Having naysaying was valuable. It made us examine every aspect of what we were doing under a microscope. We took what the resisters said very seriously and dealt with each issue. We considered more possible outcomes and put a lot more time into preparation." She also verified the plan by checking with people outside the team.

To make the naysayers more comfortable, everyone on the team got a lot of training in advance, and the naysayers ended up doing the best job.

"We got them to buy into the plan," she says, "by showing them that they could add a lot of value to it."

But What If the Team Screws Up?

It happens. Sometimes teams underestimate the time and resources they'll need. Sometimes they take a wrong tack. And sometimes members don't give a team project the attention it requires. For whatever reason, let's assume that your team just blew a deadline. The naysayers are pointing their fingers and saying, "See, we told you so."

It's time for damage control.

"To reinstill confidence," says Kordsmeier of Northwestern Mutual, "renegotiate the target, or set a new one. Realistically determine the resources you'll need. Change the makeup of the team, if necessary, to meet the revised target."

THREATENED BY NAYSAYERS

PROBLEM: Team morale is undermined by continuing negativism on the part of others in the organization.

Possible Causes	Actions to Take	Ways to Prevent
The naysayers feel their position in the organization is threatened by teams.	Nurture a core of dedicated believers on the team. Ensure that someone in management provides an ear to hear their problems and a shoulder to lean on in trying times. Invite management and the naysayers to team meetings. Chronicle the team's achievements and demonstrate how it operates. Have sponsors meet with the naysayers for dialogue on the team issue.	Provide teams with easy access to sponsors and coaches. Have management continually reinforce the organization's dedication to teams.

PROBLEM: Some members of SDWTs continue to criticize the team concept and stay aloof from working with teammates as much as possible.

Possible Causes	Actions to Take	Ways to Prevent
Organization has not backed up its commitment to teams by putting teeth into its expectations for team-based behavior.	After all reasonable efforts to convert the naysayers have been exhausted, the only choice is to move them out— but not to another team. If possible, find them a place in the organization where they can work independently.	Develop work rules that define how people will work together and lay out consequences for behaving differently.

PROBLEM: Team members insist they are independent of each other.

Possible Causes	Actions to Take	Ways to Prevent
Their functions are too specialized to allow cross-training, may even be in disagreement with each other.	Focus on their common goal and the need for teamwork behaviors where they are interdependent.	

PROBLEM: The team is bombarded by criticism from others in the organization for not meeting a goal.

Possible Causes	Actions to Take	Ways to Prevent
The expectations of team were tied up in one final goal that may have been unrealistic.	Go back to the plan and bullet every action, every short-term milestone team did meet on the way toward the ultimate goal.	Be very careful not to over-promise.
	Publicize everything accomplished so far.	Have many objectives: short term wins that you plan for and publicize, so that with each successive accomplishment the team builds credibility.
	Accept the criticism as constructive feedback. Re-examine the team's strategy to see how to improve it. Check out your approach with objective people outside the team.	Build into your plan a system for obtaining constructive feedback from interested parties all along the way.
	Invite the naysayers to join and be a part of the solution.	Keep the stakeholders advised along the way so people know ahead if a target may not be met and what team plans to do about it.
Team missed a deadline or short-term objective.	Own up to missing the target and advise the organization of what the team is doing to recoup.	
	Renegotiate the target. Make sure the team has the necessary resources and people to achieve it this time.	

He adds, "And make darn sure you meet that next target. One failure can mean you will need 8 to 10 successes to regain credibility."

To guard against failure a second time, he advises keeping stakeholders informed along the way so people know ahead of time if a deadline may not be met. If you warn them in advance, there is a better chance they will either accept your reason or help provide extra resources so you can meet the target after all.

Chapter 5

Troubled by Turnover

Whenever a valued employee leaves a traditional work unit, the unit limps along for awhile until the manager finds and trains a replacement and the manager and employees settle on the best rearrangement of the workload. It's unsettling, but people are used to it and life goes on.

When a team member leaves a close-knit team, the impact is incrementally different.

"Turnover is like a gunshot wound to a customer focus team," one team coach told Kevin Haurin of Picker International. "Every time you change personnel, team unity dies a little."

Why is the impact on a team so much more profound? Because a traditional work unit is only an organizational structure—a group of individuals joined by common reporting relationships and defined interdependencies in their functions. But a real team is an organic thing, a group of people so fused in their work that to remove one threatens the very essence of the whole.

"Teams operating at a profound level have history; they've lived through a lot together," explains Marc Bridgham of Boeing. "That shared history is a big component of teamwork. The things that stand out for people are the crises they shared and conquered—that Christmas, for example, when everybody worked overtime, doing 80 offloads in a week. It was awful but they lived through it together."

So replacing a team member is a bigger job than just locating someone with the right skills to fill the vacant shoes. It requires rebuilding the whole team from a group shattered into individuals again, each wondering, "What's

36

the new person's role? How will it change the team? How will others relate to the new person? How will the new person and others relate to me? What's my place here going to be now?"

All that on top of the usual: Can the person do the job? How are we going to get the work done now?"

Meanwhile the new person is wondering all the same things as well as: "What is this team working on? What are its goals? Will these plans work? Will anyone listen to my ideas? What do I have to do to belong here?"

A new person with self confidence and a modicum of spunk may challenge some previous decisions, causing the team to rehash old issues, often resurfacing old disagreements within the team, or tarnishing old legends: "What did you do all that overtime last Christmas for? You wouldn't have had to if you'd just . . . "

The team, with its wholeness shaken, falls back somewhere between the first two of the four stages of team development often called forming, storming, norming, and performing. Members bounce back and forth between polite, guarded interchange and frustrated, sometimes heated, struggles for control. Not until the team integrates the new person can it develop new working norms and get back into a high-performing mode.

Many teams practice effective techniques for making that happen faster. Several suggestions for both self-directed work teams and project teams follow.

Let the Team Hire Replacements

"We have a constantly changing team make-up," says Chevron team member Kristen Machen. "The only time our team has really taken some serious detours from being a highly effective team has been when new members have been added without the team having input."

Machen explains why recruitment is more successful when the team does it: "We know the skill sets needed and who could possibly fit."

Haurin of Picker International agrees. "We decided very early that teams would hire replacements," he says. "When teams have done the hiring, the new person is much better accepted than when the coach brings in a person."

Bring the New Person Up to Speed Fast

Too often new team members struggle to figure out what's happened on the team so far by picking up clues, asking repeated questions, and raising old issues. That leads to frustration for both newcomers and veterans. Sherri Lindenberg of Equitable Life suggests how to bypass that torturous period for project teams. She likes to give new team members copies of minutes of meetings, condensed to their essentials, and action points. It's critical, she maintains, to give the new person something concrete to show where you are.

Written documentation is not always enough, Lindenberg adds, especially if the team is dealing with touchy issues that members may feel uncomfortable speaking frankly about in front of someone new. Lindenberg is involved in just such a team, one dealing with diversity.

"We've had to share some sensitive things," she relates. "When we get a new person we'll have to go through it again or we won't be comfortable and the new person, won't know how we feel on some important issues." In a case like this she recommends having a couple of members meet first with the newcomer to jumpstart the person.

Mentor the Newcomer

Especially if the team lacks confidence in the new person's ability, it's helpful to pair the newcomer up with a veteran team member. Jane DeLong of Blue Cross Blue Shield of Montana says some of that company's more mature teams provide team mentors for new employees. The mentor sits with the newcomer through an orientation program that is partly computer generated, partly paper and pencil, and includes topics like "how we communicate, how we have meetings, and plans for changes in star points [specific team tasks assigned to team members, usually on a rotating basis]."

The team Kristen Machen belongs to at Chevron has a variety of team roles ranging from team leader to purchasing agent. The team designates some as major and others as minor. As soon as someone new joins the team, Machen says, the newcomer is given one of the minor roles and assigned as backup to a major one.

"We spend plenty of time mentoring," she adds, "not only technically but also in teamwork."

Guard Against New vs Old

Pairing up new and veteran members also defends against the development of a we-they syndrome if a team takes on several new members in a brief time frame. Unless they are quickly assimilated, the newcomers are likely to band together, whether it's because they feel unwelcome or because they want to press a new agenda. Seeing that happen, the veterans, still not sure about the newcomers anyway, are likely to circle the wagons defending what they've so carefully built up thus far.

When a new vs old mentality starts to surge up in a team, it is an especially critical time, says John Kordsmeier of Northwestern Mutual, to redefine the purpose of the team and each member's expected contribution to it. That encourages people, he maintains, "to see themselves as individual contributors to the team, rather than groups of new vs old."

He adds, "Many times the leader has to work with new members to make sure they understand the contributions of experienced people, to make sure people don't assume that because they are new, they are better." Or vice versa, of course.

If the veteran-newcomer division gets critical, the situation may call for team building, led by a professional facilitator, around such issues as:

■ Expectations of the team and each other.

■ Roles and responsibilities.

■ Supporting each other.

Reassign the Work Load

Unless the team finds a clone of the person who left, turnover almost always requires some shuffling of the workload in a team. Haurin of Picker International calls this task "a moment of truth for a team." The team's maturity, he says, is tested by how it redistributes work. "At a certain level of maturity," he explains, "the change is almost seamless. Team members get together and divvy up the work."

For teams that need more help, he adds, the coach should come in and help reassign the workload.

Integrating new team members poses a perfect opportunity for the team to:

■ Review objectives and reassess action plans.

■ Reassess everyone's roles and responsibilities.

■ Revise plans to make the best use of all members' capabilities.

TROUBLED BY TURNOVER

PROBLEM: Work progress is disrupted as:
- **New team member challenges team's previous decisions.**
- **Veteran members bemoan loss of member who was replaced.**
- **Team spends time rehashing old issues.**

Possible Causes	Actions to Take	Ways to Prevent
Change in team membership throws team back into Forming Stage in the Forming/Storming/Norming/Performing Cycle. Both new and veteran members are once again assessing their own and others' places on the team.	Bring new person up to speed by documenting: • What team has done so far and why. • Impact of these actions to date. • Planned next steps. Have one member meet with newcomer to review. As a team, review the action plans and reassess everyone's roles and responsibilities.	Develop Orientation Program for new members, including: • Goals and action plans. • How team communicates • Expectations of new members. • Opportunities for new members. • Work rules • Meeting practices
Team lacks confidence in new person because it had no input in selection.	Assign new person to work as backup to a veteran team member who will "mentor" the new person until the newcomer is assimilated.	Train team to recruit, interview and evaluate potential new members. Give team final selection decision or input into management's decision.

PROBLEM: Team divides into two camps, newcomers and veterans, who largely ignore each other or actively disagree.

Possible Causes	Actions to Take	Ways to Prevent
Veterans threatened by change and/or Newcomers arrived with different agendas and/or Insufficient attention paid to assimilating newcomers into the group.	Pair each newcomer with a veteran on project tasks or in team roles. Facilitate teambuilding event, built around expectations of team and each other, roles/responsibilities, support for each other.	Periodically conduct activities to reassess and improve level of teamwork.

PROBLEM: Team is missing some competencies that existed in the original group.

Possible Causes	Actions to Take	Ways to Prevent
Replacements chosen not for their skills and knowledge but on some other basis: availability, friendship, perhaps for political reasons. Team is unable to find a replacement with all the skills of the person who left.	To get skilled replacements: • Identify and document missing competencies. • Determine if they are needed permanently or for a specific time. • Identify where the skills exist in the organization. • *Project team:* invite people with needed skills to join team for required time. • *SDWT:* use documentation to press for additional team member(s) or negotiate with other units to use their capabilities.	When hiring for SDWT, give team a role in determining skills needed and in selecting new hires. For long-term project teams, rotate membership in a systematic fashion to ensure you don't lose a great deal of experience and capability all at once.

■ Identify remaining skill gaps caused by the former member's departure.

■ Determine ways to fill those gaps—e.g. bringing in a temporary or part-time member, sharing the resources of another part of the organization, developing the skills within the existing group.

And Now the Good News

Many companies using self-directed work teams report that reduced turnover is one of the benefits of SDWTs. As Alec McCommon of FedEx says, "In teams, people like the culture better and don't leave as often for a small raise."

Machen of Chevron sums up why: "I am not told to check my brain at the door and do as I am told. I am directly responsible for what I will be working on in the future. The satisfaction of having a job that I love with people I enjoy working with cannot be measured in a paycheck."

Chapter 6

Tensions, Rivalries Among Team Members

"Teams are like families." Almost to a person, the team experts interviewed for this Management Briefing began their comments on intra-team conflict with that statement. Often it was accompanied by a sigh, suggesting that in teams, as in families, periodic eruptions and more frequent undercurrents were something you just had to learn to live with.

As Kevin Haurin of Picker International says, "Families argue, but they love each other." Ironically, it is that very familiarity that creates the kind of atmosphere where emotional explosions occur.

"As teams mature," Haurin points out, "members become more open with each other." Where once they were cautious about stepping on each other's toes and tactful to avoid any chance of hurting someone else, now they skip the niceties and blurt out what they think, expecting to be understood and, if necessary, forgiven. And usually they are. Seeming criticism that fellow team members would once have taken personally is now likely to give rise to a shrug with a casual, "Oh you know Mary. She always talks like that. She doesn't mean anything by it."

But over time, small irritants can fester until the atmosphere gets pretty tense. And on any given day, tempers can fly.

"Coaches have reported team members getting and screaming at each other," Haurin divulges.

Screaming is not always so bad. "We teach team members from the beginning that it's all right to be emotional because you really care about what needs to be done," Haurin explains. But if being emotional about what needs to be done crosses over into being disrespectful toward another person, that's not all right.

"We tell them to focus on the issue, not on each other," he stresses. "Because they need each other's help," he adds, "they usually are careful to retain respect for each other."

When disagreements flare and voices rise over a work issue, the least invasive approach is for fellow team members to deal with the problem either in a team meeting or off-line (one on one between a combatant and a calmer colleague at a quieter moment). If that doesn't work, the leader of a project team or coach of an SDWT may need to step in. In accelerating order, there are several approaches to try.

Is Performance Affected?

Letting off steam can be cathartic. It can even be the jolt a team needs to free it from a mental logjam that is stifling progress. So if the behavior does nothing worse than rattle the coffee cups and make fellow team members momentarily uncomfortable, the best approach is to ignore it or defuse it with humor.

But if the behavior of one or two people disrupts the team's work, drawing colleagues into the melee or shutting off contributions by the less uninhibited members of the team, someone needs to address it.

Who Beards the Lion?

The team. The best approach is for the team to deal with its own miscreants. If the unacceptable behavior takes place in a team meeting, someone on the team should interrupt on the spot, calling attention to the discrepancy between the disruptive behavior and the team's ground rules. For a team with no documented rules for working together, this is a good jumping off point to create a set. Rather than focus on one person's acting out, the team can codify its working rules, defining productive behaviors and identifying behaviors it will not tolerate.

Dealing with Explosive Behavior

Ask Yourself:	What To Do
Does it affect the performance of the team?	No →Ignore it.
Yes ↓	
Has the team itself tried to change its member's behavior?	No →Team addresses member's behavior based on team ground rules. If it has none, this is a good time to create them.
Yes ↓	
Is this behavior an ongoing pattern (as opposed to an isolated incident)?	No →Call a break in the activity that precipitated the explosive behavior. Before reconvening get the combatant(s)' agreement to desist.
Yes ↓	
Is the behavior the result of a disagreement over the best answer to a specific work problem?	No →If conflict is based less on substance than on personality or style, use Myers-Briggs or other work style assessment instrument to validate different styles.
	Yes →Facilitate team problem solving.

If members are uncomfortable dealing together with individuals' behavior, an alternate approach is for a well-respected member to meet one on one with the offenders when tempers have died down and calmer reason prevails.

Team leader or coach. Sometimes an SDWT will resist dealing with personnel problems just because it is reluctant to handle an unpleasant responsibility. In that case, the coach's best approach is a supportive but firm,

"I'll be there to help you, but you need to handle this." If the team does not have the skills to address the problem effectively, then the coach should set up training for the team—so it's ready next time—and step in to resolve the current issue so the team can move on.

Is It an Isolated Incident or a Recurring Problem?

If the explosive behavior is a devastating, but uncommon, incident, then the coach's best approach is the same one outlined above for team members. If you are a team leader or a coach presiding over a meeting where a sudden fracas occurs, start by taking the advice of Sherri Lindenberg of Equitable Life: Call a break. That disrupts the momentum, and when people come back, they'll probably be ready to focus calmly on the meeting agenda.

But if one or two team members exhibit a pattern of temperamental behavior that is affecting the ability of others to perform, you've got a bigger job on your hands.

What's Precipitating the Behavior?

How you approach the issue will depend upon what is causing it. If the team is wrestling with a significant work problem and the frayed tempers arise from honest disagreements about the best solution, the real cause of the situation may be that the team has no structured method of team problem solving that surfaces a range of options, allows everyone to be heard on the issue, and concludes with consensus on the best way to proceed. You may facilitate a structured problem solving session yourself or bring in a skilled facilitator. But the team will win big in the long run if you help it get the training to do its own consensus problem solving in the future.

Is It a Clash of Style?

Whether tensions erupt into overt clashes or stay at that uncomfortable level where people just don't get along very well, the cause is often style, not substance.

"One of the things I see that causes tension in teams is the difference between introverted and extroverted people," says Marc Bridgham, organization development consultant at Boeing. "When you have some people who process by reflecting on everything and speak only when they are ready and other people who think out loud and bounce ideas off each other, you have a real two-party thing going on."

The loud folks get louder and the quiet folks get quieter. The quiet ones think their vociferous colleagues are dominating and the loud ones think their reflective teammates are holding back.

"We use Myers-Briggs and other assessments to put the differences on the table and say, 'Ya, it's real. You are different. It's not a values thing.' People process things differently, and that's OK."

When people understand style differences, they find a way to kid about their own and others' behaviors. At Boeing, Bridgham notes, there are a lot of very task directed engineers. When they catch themselves being short with others, they'll say, "Oh ya, there's me being directive again."

They also learn to value others' qualities. Bridgham tells of a team that struggled over a change in leader. The first one had been extroverted, chummy, articulate, and very well liked by the team. The new one was totally the opposite: very quiet and analytical, hardly volunteering two words together. For awhile that caused some real tension within the team. The members assumed the new leader did not like them, didn't trust them, and didn't want to be there. After doing Myers-Briggs with the two leaders, Bridgham helped the team realize the difference was only one of style. The new leader was on their side and was happy to help them when they took their problems to him.

Sean Stevens, of the Fortune 500 health products company, uses a team assessment instrument, as well as Chris Argyris' Ladder of Inference[1] to help people understand how they make observations, attribute motivation, and take actions based on assumptions rather than facts.

"I get examples of why John doesn't trust Pat," Stevens explains, and we find out that ascriptions are made to behavior that are not necessarily true."

Focus on the Objective

Kristin Machen of Chevron remembers being party to a clash of temperaments. "Two of us were at each other's throats," she recalls. "We had very different styles. The other person is more creative, a free thinker. I'm much more of a process person."

Machen couldn't avoid her nemesis. Not only did they share a team role, portfolio manager, but at that time he was the team leader. At her wits

[1] Senge et al, *The Fifth Discipline Fieldbook.* New York: Doubleday, 1994.

end, she approached her Center of Excellence manager, John Fair, and said, "I can't do this." Valuing them both, Fair asked them to try to work out their differences.

"What we did," she explains, "was figure out our main objective and make sure we stayed focused on it." They asked themselves what they were trying to accomplish. The answer for both of them was the same: build a portfolio. That required both thinking two years down the road and thinking five years ahead

"I was more two years," she says, "He was more five. We realized we complemented each other and came up with a balance of both."

"We still get into heated discussions," she adds, but they're not personal. We found we could focus on each other's positives, rather than negatives."

When Conflicts Escalate

If all associates worked out their own conflicts the way Machen and her colleague did, team leaders and coaches would have an easier job. Unfortunately, there are cases when someone has to step in, often at the request of the combatants themselves and sometimes petitioned by other team members who are suffering from fallout.

If team building around work styles doesn't resolve a specific conflict between two individuals, the leader or coach will probably have to meet with them away from the rest of the team.

"I try to meet with them separately," says Jean Maier of Northwestern Mutual Life. Sometimes she'll cut a project team meeting short because of unresolved hostility between members.

Privately, she says, "I call the person on it. I'll ask, 'What's going on here? I sensed you were really angry at _____.'" As a project team leader, her solution of last resort is to ask to have a team member replaced.

A slightly different approach worked for Duncan Crundwell of Detroit, CEO of Solid State Logic Organ Systems, a British company. Formerly manager of a company plant in England, he implemented self-directed work teams there.

Some of the personnel conflicts surprised him. "In a traditional organization," he notes, "people hold in their emotions. In teams, emotions come out. People may come to you and say, 'The others don't like me.'"

When he saw conflicts getting in the way of performance, his approach was to call a meeting with *both* belligerents with certain ground rules:

TENSIONS, RIVALRIES AMONG TEAM MEMBERS		
PROBLEM: Overt hostility, vociferous disagreements erupt in meetings and workplace.		
Possible Causes	Actions to Take	Ways to Prevent
Members have become familiar enough with each other to be frank, disagree openly, and express negative feelings	Differentiate between highly emotional responses to issues and attacks on individuals. Tolerate the former as long as work progress continues.	Develop and document Rules for Working Together. Schedule periodic reviews, updates of Rules.
	Keep the team focused on its main objective.	
	Identify team's customer and relate all behaviors to meeting the customer's needs.	
	Conduct teambuilding focused on what each member contributes to meeting the objective and satisfying the customer.	
Members may be frozen into opposing positions on an unresolved issue.	Raise unresolved issues and: • Air and give respect to all points of view. • Come to consensus if possible. • Get commitment to contain differences.	

- Each could speak only to him, not to the other.

- Only one could speak at a time.

The purpose was to set them up to listen to each other, rather than think about formulating responses. "I tried very hard," he says, "to teach people the skills of looking at something from someone else's point of view."

It's useful, he reports, to ask each person to:

- Put yourself in the other person's shoes.

- Think of what the other person has seen you do and say.

- Ask yourself what you'd do under those circumstances.

PROBLEM: Ongoing conflict between two or more members.		
Possible Causes	**Actions to Take**	**Ways to Prevent**
Unacknowledged personality or work-style differences.	Do teambuilding using Myers Briggs or other instrument that surfaces and validates personal style differences.	Periodically revisit personal styles in team meetings.
Battle for position in team's real or perceived hierarchy.	To deal with overt or covert personal attacks (in accelerating order): • Have the team handle the problem, with a facilitator if necessary. • Meet separately with each party to get commitment to more appropriate behavior. • Bring all conflicting parties together to resolve problem. • With the team's agreement, remove one or more members.	Train team in Conflict Management. Agree on consequences for breaking the Rules for Working Together.

When you convert a work unit to a team-based organization, Crundwell found, "you go from being a manager controlling an operation to being a person who is putting out fires and teaching people how to get along with each other."

Chapter 7

Individual Performance Problems

Most people will go out of their way not to let their teammates down. So as self directed work teams jell, some performance problems decrease without anyone needing to address them directly.

Duncan Crundwell of Solid State Logic Organ Systems recalls that when teams took hold in his British plant, the sick record improved enormously. "People in fairly junior jobs who didn't feel like getting up in the morning used to just call in sick," he says, "but when they were on a team they realized the impact of that on other people."

Peer pressure is a potent force. But when that pressure alone is not enough to keep a team member's performance from slipping, a team may address the situation with one (or some combination) of three approaches: cover up, complain, or confront.

Covering Up

While team members occasionally cover up for a poorly performing teammate because they don't want to see a buddy get punished, more likely they do it to save the team's skin. They take over the slacker's work because it's the only way they know to keep team performance up to par. While pitching in to cover a teammate's work can solve a temporary problem—if, for example, a person is thrown off course by family troubles—it's a poor long-term solution, one that is bound to lead to resentment and burnout.

Complaining

For some teams, self management loses its rosy glow when what needs managing is a poor performing teammate. So they complain to management about the miscreant and demand that management *do something*. While most experienced team coaches are willing to provide guidance to a team that is not yet skilled at dealing with such problems, they see their proper role as:

- Training teams to handle performance problems on their own.

- Serving as counselor to the team leader and others who will confront the poor performer.

So they are likely to tell team members who complain that a colleague is not pulling his load, "I'm here to help you, but you have to take care of this."

Confronting the Problem

When it's clear that the under-performing team member lacks the skill to do the job, many teams have ways to deal with that. They use a variety of good techniques:

- Set up a buddy system with a skilled coworker.

- Assign one or more team members to do on-the-job coaching.

- Arrange for the unskilled person to get formal training.

- Develop job aids to guide a teammate through unfamiliar tasks.

- Reassign tasks so the person is doing something she has the skills to do.

What's more difficult for most teams to solve is a situation when it's apparent that the person can do the job but, for whatever reason, chooses not to.

Confronted with someone like that, team members are going to be very conscious of the fact they have to work side by side with that person. It's going to be a pretty uncomfortable workplace if the person gets angry at them. There's even the possibility that some teammates will side with the accused person, blaming the confronters for raising the team's tension level. Team coaches can help members realize that, while confrontation may be uncomfortable, their discomfort will be even greater if they do nothing.

Effective performance counseling requires skill, so teams need training and coaching before one team member or the entire team takes on the task of counseling an under-performing teammate.

Team Counseling

If the team decides on a team counseling session, it will need a facilitator. The team leader may assume the role if she has the skills. Or the coach may do it or bring in a professional facilitator from outside the team.

Before they begin, team members need to know:

- That it's OK to confront a colleague, and it's possible to do it without stripping the person of his self-respect and dignity.

- How to give specific, objective feedback that is descriptive, not accusatory.

- How to listen objectively to someone else's point of view, and how to present their own views noncombatively.

- How to paraphrase—the skill that clarifies what's been said, dispels misunderstandings, shows respect, and proves you've been listening.

For the team counseling session, a typical agenda includes:

- Facilitator defines the performance problem.

- Team members describe the impact on the team. That helps the poor performer understand the consequences of his actions.

- Poor performer gets the first opportunity to suggest a solution.

- Team members recommend additional actions to take, if necessary, until they come up with a solution that satisfies their needs.

- Team gets the commitment of the poor performer.

■ Team determines sanctions if the poor performer does not meet the team's terms.

During or immediately after the counseling session, it's important to get the terms and the commitment in writing. The written agreement provides a reminder if memories get fuzzy, standards against which to measure performance improvement, and documentation for management if the situation reaches the formal discipline stage.

Suffering from the impact of a team member who wasn't performing up to par, one production team addressed the problem with the person at a team meeting and established a performance improvement plan. The team set hourly and daily production goals for the person.

The experience was difficult for everyone, but the person's performance improved. And so did that of a couple of others on the team whose performance was borderline.

Giving Feedback

The essence of effective counseling is giving good feedback. When it began its conversion to SDWTs, one Bell Atlantic division taught team members the following feedback rules:

For the person giving feedback: Describe your feelings, the person's behavior, and the impact of that behavior on you personally. Put all this in the form of an I-statement. For example, "I'm frustrated when you don't come to work on time, because there are customers waiting and I don't get my other work done."

For the person getting feedback: Say nothing about it for 24 hours. Then decide what to do about it.

After 24 hours, practitioners discover, much of the defensiveness dissolves, but the lessons of the feedback remain.

Taking Disciplinary Action

If a performance problem reaches the disciplinary stage teams in most companies turn it over to management. "We asked teams how they would approach a situation where an individual was not meeting standards," reports Haurin of Picker International. "Would they replace them or work with them

INDIVIDUAL PERFORMANCE PROBLEMS

PROBLEM: Team members inform team leader or coach that one member is not pulling his/her weight.

Possible Causes	Actions to Take	Ways to Prevent
Underperforming team member does not know what is expected of him/her.	Confirm by observation and documentation that team member is underperforming. Team leader or teammates explain what is required of the underperforming member.	Have up-to-date Team Charter, action plans, and job descriptions that detail the tasks to be done and the skills required, as well as the roles and responsibilities of team members.
Underperforming team member does not have skills to do the tasks.	In SDWT, provide coaching by coworker or team coach or training in classroom or via other media.	Provide coaching and training before putting people into roles. Periodically reassess skill needs and team members' abilities. In SDWT, create, monitor and update development plans for all team members.
Underperforming team member is capable but unwilling to do the tasks.	Mature SDWT's: • Counsel the poor performer. • Establish expectations. • Document progress. • If necessary, provide documentation to management for disciplinary action.	Train SDWTs to handle individual performance problems through team counseling, constructive feedback, and holding poor performers accountable for improvement. In project team, periodically devote meeting time to reassessing everyone's continuing commitment to project. Release and replace unwilling members before their attitude affects the team.

to solve the problem? Unanimously, they said work with the person. That's a strength and a weakness."

A strength, because it confirms their commitment to supporting each other and developing people. A weakness, however, if it means they are reluctant to take tough actions when necessary. "We've never given the responsibility for firing to any team," he adds.

PROBLEM: Team members take on extra workloads to cover for underperforming teammate.		
Possible Causes	**Actions to Take**	**Ways to Prevent**
Team members may be: • Afraid one person's poor performance will reflect on entire team. • Unwilling to "rat" on a coworker. • Unwilling to be perceived of as "bad guys." • Convinced it is the only way to keep team performance at required level.	Encourage the team to address the issue at a team meeting with agenda items such as: • Impact of extra work on members • Documented imbalance among members of work performed, • Team's expectations of all members • Violation of team charter and groundrules if these exist • Steps team will take to address the issue.	Train teams to deal with performance problems. Make outside facilitators available to help teams handle sensitive meetings.

In companies with extensive experience with SDWTs, teams are expected to handle much of the discipline themselves, short of dismissing the person. A typical sequence of steps includes:

■ Discussion of the problem with the employee by the team or a team representative.

■ Oral warning, with 30 days to improve performance.

■ Written notice, drafted by the team and approved by the manager.

■ Recommendation of probation, at which point management takes over.

But those are steps for an extreme situation. One of the best things about teams, members and coaches agree, is that performance problems seldom reach that stage.

Chapter 8

Growing Resentment: "I Don't Get Paid for This"

Being chosen to participate in a cross-functional project team is pretty exciting for an employee. Just being selected is a form of recognition and the project is often bigger, broader, and higher profile than an individual job. But if the employee ends up spending full workdays on his regular job, then devoting evenings and weekends to the project work, the glow of being singled out for something special begins to fade. That's when the employee may start to wonder, or to complain out loud, "What am I doing this for? I don't get paid for this."

Increasingly the organizational response to that complaint is, "Oh yes, you do. That's exactly what you get paid for. There's no place in the organization for someone who can just do one job."

Sherri Lindenberg of Equitable Life says, "In our environment right now, the message is, You've got two jobs. Figure out a way to do them both."

Because project team work is so important, she adds, "It's often your old job that needs to be done off the side of your desk now, rather than vice versa."

At Northwestern Mutual Life, project teams are so thoroughly entrenched that no one remembers working any other way. The company has two policies that eliminate the "no extra pay" complaint, explains John Kordsmeier:

First, the norm is for people to work within defined work times. So if they are on a project team, that work substitutes for—rather than is added to—other tasks they would be doing.

Second, says Kordsmeier, "We try to factor team contributions into the formal performance management system. And we have a recognition program where anyone can give a gift to another person who has gone above and beyond the call of duty."

Intrinsic Rewards

In SDWTs, the extra work is twofold: maintaining the team relationship and running the business—what the supervisor used to do. For team members, the main payoff is intrinsic, says Marc Bridgham. "It's the ability to influence my environment, to have a voice in problem solving and decision making about things that affect me."

Steve Nielsen of FedEx agrees, at least for the short term. "If you can help me see where I am really having an impact on the goal—for us that's moving goods faster than anyone else—that's going to help me have a better feeling and I may not need that extra compensation."

Sometimes, he points out, the rewards people really want are not pay raises. "When we asked what it would take to have 100 percent delivery in the morning," he reports, "the first response we got was a special parking space. Another was a day off."

But, Nielsen believes, companies will need to provide more tangible rewards in the long run. "People like to pit themselves against a challenge," he says, "but once they've proved themselves, they'll start to ask, 'What's in it for me?' The Hawthorne effect will carry you about two and a half years."

If his numbers are right, that means the pay issue is very likely to rise up as another "sophomore slump" team problem.

Some Solutions

Pay extra for team roles. At a Texas plant, Boeing has a pay differential for some team roles, such as team facilitator. Since these roles are rotated, everyone gets a shot at the extra pay—and the extra work.

Split up the responsibilities so the extra load is small enough to do during normal work hours. The extra pay problem arose at Picker International with an additional twist. A delegate—a role with wide responsi-

GROWING RESENTMENT: I DON'T GET PAID FOR THIS

PROBLEM: As SDWTs mature and take on more supervisory responsibilities, members object to doing extra work without extra pay.

Possible Causes	Actions to Take	Ways to Prevent
There is no apparent reward for performing additional tasks.	Clarify the link between new team skills and career development. Facilitate team discussions comparing the "old way" to the team way to reinforce the non-monetary benefits of belonging to teams. Provide many kinds of non-monetary recognition to teams and team members.	Implement a formal Recognition Program that honors teams and individual team members for their accomplishments. Build learning and performing team tasks into individual objective setting and performance management. Build a monetary reward for team tasks into the compensation system.
Team tasks—especially administrative ones—fall too heavily on one or two people, overburdening them.	Reassess the administrative workload, pare it down and redistribute it in small enough chunks that it can all be done in normal work hours.	Develop a "star point" system and rotate team tasks at periods determined by each team.

PROBLEM: Members of long term project teams complain about time and effort they've devoted for no extra pay.

Possible Causes	Actions to Take	Ways to Prevent
Work on project teams is not incorporated into performance management or compensation systems.	Stage a recognition event to rejuvenate enthusiasm.	Include work on team in individual annual objectives and monitor through performance management system. Incorporate incentive compensation for team contributions in compensation system.
Burnout.	Say "thank you" and release them, encouraging them to find replacements.	Establish terms for membership and rotate people in and out.

bilities including representing the team in a variety of situations—added up his extra hours and approached management. "Here are the hours I'm spending," he said. "I want to get paid for this. And because I'm doing it at night, after taking care of customers during the day, I want to get paid *overtime* for it!"

"We never asked them to do this work on their own time," Haurin says, but the fact remained that this team member couldn't get the additional work done during the day.

Haurin and his colleagues solved the problem by splitting the delegate's job into smaller pieces and sharing them among more team members so they could easily be completed during the working day.

Link the new team skills to career development. In a team-based organization, expectations of climbing a promotional ladder are definitely diminished, but opportunities exist for lateral movement and pay increases for increased skills. Help team members see how adding the team roles to their resume increases their chances of growing within and outside the organization.

Chapter 9

Slow Pace of Change In the Organization

"They called the department a team and the manager a team leader but nothing really changed," bemoaned a supervisor trying to become a team coach in an organization that had declared itself team-based but was resisting the change throughout.

It's not an unusual situation. Hoping to reap the rewards they read about in the literature on teams, the people at the top announce a reorganization into SDWTs. And they think their work is done; they provide no leadership for the change. Down on the front lines, employees react with a cynical shrug. In between are threatened layers of managers who cling to their hierarchical claim to position and authority.

Or as Mil Rosseau of Autonoom in Belgium puts it, "Some managers confuse drawing a new organization with a change process."

When an organization's actions regarding teams lag behind its words, change agents address the situation on three fronts:

Management, to involve them and to demonstrate what's in it for them.
Teams, to ensure they are truly working as SDWTs, not cleverly disguised little hierarchies.
Reward system, to develop an appropriate balance of incentives for team behaviors and individual initiative.

60

When Management Drags Its Heels

When companies flatten into SDWT-based organizations, middle managers often get left out in the cold. They're shuffled about, instructed to become coaches—but sometimes with neither training nor support—or left shakily in place on the organization chart but with no meaningful job descriptions.

They can join the movement or they can resist it. When they resist, often by not sharing information or refusing to work on a peer basis with team members, they can create a formidable obstacle to team success.

Mil Rosseau confesses that when he helped organize SDWTs at DVV, a European insurance company, "we forgot about middle managers." The company had been very hierarchical, he says. The credo was, "The boss tells me or I do nothing." Then new management turned the organization around 180 degrees with self-directed work teams, jeopardizing middle managers' power base.

Rosseau explains how DVV recouped. Meeting with the middle managers, Rosseau and the company leaders did the following:

- Listened while middle managers listed all their problems with the new approach.

- Gave answers as much as possible.

- Put them on existing teams as technical specialists, recognizing the technical expertise that probably boosted them into management in the first place.

- Invited them to start up new teams, specifically to speed up organizational processes.

"While 50 to 60 of them had been reluctant to get into teaming," says Rosseau, "now only four or five are still resisting."

Getting First-Line Managers on Board

At first glance, what first-line managers see when they look at their new job description is that they are still accountable for the same or increased output, but they've lost their authority to make it happen. Is it any wonder that some of them will do everything they can to slow down the process to transform the organization? Often in their own work areas they succeed, for months or even years.

"It's essential to get first line managers on board," confirms Kevin Haurin of Picker International. "As coaches they need to focus the teams on what needs to be done."

The coaches need coaching too, as well as training in the skills for their new job, and forums to share problems and solutions with each other. Haurin sets up periodic coaches' conference calls after collecting from them the issues they are struggling with. "All I try to do," he says, "is to facilitate a situation where they can talk and learn from each other."

Is It a Team or a Work Group?

Especially if the coach is reluctant to give up supervisory control, the team itself can cling to the old comfortable pattern of following the boss's orders.

At Chevron Petroleum Technology Company, says John Fair, "Part of the role of the Center of Excellence manager is to figure out if they are behaving as teams or not."

That's easy to do, he says, with a set of questions that includes: "How do you resolve disputes within the team? How do you solve problems? Who has what role? How are roles decided upon?"

When Boeing started SDWTs, says Marc Bridgham, it used several methods to set them up. In some parts of the company it provided only core guidelines, allowing the teams to figure out what variations on the theme worked best for them. Bridgham is a strong advocate of this approach but admits there is a danger that people will say, 'OK, I'm just going to change the names.'"

To combat that, he explains, the company uses people as pathfinders and models. "After a couple of years we went out and found examples and shared those throughout the company, highlighting how much money they saved or what disaster they averted. It's important to recognize and reward those people."

He adds, "You have to be careful not to reward those who simply changed the letterhead—where the chart looks good but people on the floor know better."

Fair agrees. "If we see that a team is building facades," he says, "their pay suffers."

Rewarding Teamwork

At Chevron Petroleum Technology Company, 50 percent of team members' pay increases is dependent upon individual performance and 50 percent on team contribution, including not only performance against goals but also development and application of team processes.

Finding the best balance of individual versus team recognition is an issue all team-based organizations struggle with in their performance appraisal systems. If appraisals focus on individuals rather than teams, what happens to the motivation to work together? But when ratings are team-based, resentment rises when high performing team members feel their less industrious teammates are getting a free ride.

When TACOM-TARDEC reorganized into SDWTs, it eliminated individual performance evaluations in favor of a single team evaluation. A key input into each team's rating was an assessment by its customers on how well the team achieved objectives established jointly by the team and the customers. The organization was confident that the system would encourage the teams themselves to deal with "freeloaders riding on the coattails of others."

The process, says Michael Bailey, "brought associates closer to the customer and reflected TACOM-TARDEC's absolute commitment to the teaming structure." But two years later, in response to a task force recommendation, it changed the system, re-injecting individual ratings. Now associates have individual as well as team objectives and if one associate fails to meet hers, a teammate who meets or exceeds his won't be penalized.

Driving Change from the Top

Ultimately, without visible upper management involvement, building and maintaining a team-based organization will always be an uphill battle. John Fair has some final words of advice to senior managers: "You have to have some kind of conscience to keep you connected to what's happening—a consultant, perhaps, or a process for getting feedback from the people. It can be painful, but if you can address what they're upset about, you add to your credibility."

SLOW PACE OF CHANGE IN ORGANIZATION

PROBLEM: In team-based organization: Management continues to send directives via former supervisors and expect supervisors to make decisions and direct work.

Possible Causes	Actions to Take	Ways to Prevent
Middle managers had no input into decision to restructure into teams, view teams as threat to their power base. Managers are accountable for their units' success and have no skills for ensuring this in any but traditional way.	*By upper management:* • Reinforce organization's commitment to teams. • Address issue of managers' career paths under new structure • Invite middle managers' input into improving team structure. • Clarify managers' accountability for success of teams • Provide training in managing teams. *By teams:* Build an inventory of improvements in work unit results under team structure.	Regularly readdress all the issues under "Actions to Take."
Compensation is still based on individual rather than team contributions.	*By upper management:* • Recognize managers and supervisors for team successes using spot bonuses or nonmonetary rewards. • Include measurable goals for team processes and results in annual objectives for managers and supervisors. *By teams:* Use upward recognition—gift, thank you letter, lunch, etc.— to show appreciation for any positive step by management.	Build incentives for team processes and results into compensation system at all levels in organization.

PROBLEM: Team members still expect former supervisors to tell them what to do and provide resources, especially for difficult, risky, or sensitive problems.

Possible Causes	Actions to Take	Ways to Prevent
Members believe that organization is not committed to operating in self-directed teams.	Provide former supervisors with training and incentives for moving into coaching role. Provide teams with training, coaching and continuous support, and require them to make and execute decisions. Reward success; treat failures as learning experiences.	Establish a schedule for teams to learn management tasks and assume responsibilities. Reward teams for reaching each level of maturity.

Chapter 10

An Ounce of Prevention

. . . Well, maybe it's more like a pound. But one thing's certain: As much time as you put in at the outset to define your objectives, roles and responsibilities, ground rules, time frame, and schedules—you'll save incrementally more later by avoiding pitfalls and problems. This is equally true for both SDWTs and project teams.

But this chapter is not about what you shoulda done. It's about what you can do now to prevent future problems, if not instantly to solve the ones you are confronting today. In fact, many team experts agree, when you are confronted with a problem is often the best time to develop a team charter, work out team ground rules, and decide how you will monitor your adherence to them and their continuing applicability. This is when you know from experience, not theory, what they need to contain and what issues they need to resolve before those issues turn into team crises.

If you haven't done these things already, start now.

Write a Team Charter

At the very least, it should describe the team's mission and specific objectives, who the key players are, their roles and responsibilities, team tasks, and interdependencies if any. Project teams should also identify team sponsors and define the time commitment. Some charters also include ground rules, but other teams prefer to separate these into another document. At the end of this chapter is an abbreviated sample team charter, one provided by a self-directed work team at Blue Cross Blue Shield of Montana.

Working Rules

Whether you include these in the charter or develop them separately, these commit the team to acceptable rules of engagement for everyone on the team. Mil Rosseau compiled the sample list below from rules set by teams in several European companies, but most of them would be equally applicable to teams anywhere:

- Passive bilingualism (especially important in Belgium: each team member speaks his/her own language and does not adapt to the language of the speaker/majority);
- Meeting sessions of 45 minutes, followed by a short break of ±10 minutes (for teams where availability to customers is important);
- In a brainstorm, everybody has to come up with at least one contribution;
- Rules on smoking during the meeting;
- Switching of team roles on a regular basis;
- No negative remarks without giving at least one possible solution;
- Confidentiality on all issues until a formal communication plan is worked out;
- Every meeting has a "De Bono Black Hat" session (paying attention to the worst case scenario).

Revisit the Charter and Working Rules Regularly

The team charter and working rules are neither dead documents nor carved in stone, so don't file them away in the bottom of a drawer nor cast them in bronze (or lucite). Schedule regular meetings to revisit them and ask yourselves:

- Are we sticking to them?
- Do they still apply?

- Do we need to modify them, add items, remove some?
- Are these still the right people?
- Do we need to include any additional interdependencies?
- How can we make them better?

Review and Update Job Descriptions

Written job descriptions are often as out of date as last decade's hairstyles. Who cares? Nobody looks at them anyway. That's often the truth, until someone wants an excuse to get out of an unpleasant task or shift an accountability, or a new manager wants to reassign a team member. Then, unless those job descriptions are up to date, they can be a powerful document for turning back the clock. So pull them out of the bottom drawer and rewrite them to reflect team responsibilities.

Training

Effective teams don't develop out of wishful thinking, they depend upon highly developed skills for working together. So make sure the team gets training and continued coaching in meeting facilitation, team problem solving, conflict management, working with people with different styles, and any other interpersonal, functional, or administrative skills your team needs to block many problems from ever happening and nip the rest while they are mere irritants, long before they reach the hair-tearing stage.

BILLINGS SERVICE TEAM CHARTER*

Team Purpose

The Billings Service Team is a group of individuals that take pride in being a dedicated and empowered Team, utilizing their experience and expertise to provide excellent service to internal and external customers of Blue Cross Blue Shield of Montana.

Ground Rules

1 Celebrate successes, have fun, share food—PARTY!
2 Anything disclosed in Team meetings that could be considered sensitive or confidential in nature, should remain within the Team.
3 Build trust and loyalty with each other.
4 Open Communication.
5 Disagreements between Team Members are to be handled on a one-to-one basis. If unable to resolve the issue, it should be addressed with the Team.
6 Choose not to take things personally/realize and accept disagreements.
7 Encourage one another.
8 Show respect, courtesy and value differences of all Team Members.
9 Encourage Involvement of all Team Members and balance participation.
10 Allow the person who is speaking to finish.
11 Ask for help as often as needed.
12 Individual Team Members will cover for each other as needed.
13 Attempt to display a positive attitude.
14 Support Team decisions.
15 Ground rules will be added and/or changed as needed.
16 All Team Members are responsible for monitoring Ground Rules by using Key Principles.

Tasks

- Team Members will rotate facilitation of team meetings.
- Team Members will attend all scheduled meetings.
- Team Members will take advantage of available cross training.
- Team Members will follow Corporate Vision and Values.

---

* Source: Christine Burbank, Team Coach, Billings Service Team. Reprinted with permission.

- Team Members will consistently follow Team Ground Rules.
- Team Members will be accountable to NMIS.
- Team Members will be accountable to meet production levels.
- Team Members will strive to move through the continuum.

Boundaries:
- **Team Leader:**

  Serves as a coordinator between the Service Team and Senior Management. Facilitates learning, decision making, provides direction, mentoring and motivation to the Team....

- **Team Coach:**

  Reports to the Team Leader and serves as a liaison between the Team, the Team Leader and other teams. Facilitates learning and decision making, provides mentoring and motivation....

  Team Members:

  Team Members report to the Team Coach and are responsible for the Team's production. They can: authorize expenditures up to $100.00; can schedule meetings, vacations and time off as long as the phones are covered; determine cross training needs in accordance with established plan; can arrange flex times in accordance with established guidelines; can order medical records as needed, can mentor new Team Members; can pursue information from other sources outside of the Team; can apply grace days for groups in accordance with guidelines; can override timely filing in accordance with guidelines; can implement process improvements; can compile and evaluate data on quality, productivity and timeliness....

Team Meetings:
- When ....Every Tuesday from 8:00 to 9:00 am
                                Every other Thursday from 8:00 to 9:00 am
- Where.........................In team work area or designated area
- Who ....All team members
- Guidelines ....Attendance is mandatory
                                Balanced participation by all team members
                                Agendas—distributed by facilitator by 3:00 PM the day before the meeting

Measures of Success:

- Meeting and/or exceeding NMIS goals
- Meeting and/or exceeding our Team's goals
- Ability to tie Team success to the Company's Vision and Values
- Staying within our Team budget
- Being pro-active with planning
- Closing issues—they then become accomplishments

About the Author

Donna Deeprose is a training consultant and business writer who specializes in executive, management, and employee development. She is the author of How to Recognize and Reward Employees and Team Coach: Vital New Skills for Supervisors & Managers in a Team Environment (AMACOM), as well as numerous articles on management and leadership topics.

She lives in New York City.

For additional copies of **Recharge Your Team—Keep Them Going and Going...**

CALL: **800-262-9699** (518-891-1500 outside the U.S.). FAX: **518-891-0368**. E-MAIL: **cust_serv@amanet.org**. WRITE: **Management Briefings, AMA Publication Services, P.O. Box 319, Saranac Lake, NY 12983**.

Ask for Stock # 2366XACZ. **$12.95/$11.65 AMA Members**. A multiple-copy discount is available. Call for details. Applicable sales tax and shipping & handling will be added to your order.

OTHER MANAGEMENT BRIEFINGS OF INTEREST

The Computer Time Bomb: How to Keep the Century Date Change from Killing Your Organization—Outlines the steps you—as a manager—can and must take today to correct this Y2K problem. Includes corporate profiles, case studies, and a 15-point self-test to see whether your organization is prepared to deal with this problem. Stock #2365XACZ, $24.95/22.45 AMA Members.

A Better Place to Work: A New Sense of Motivation Leading to Higher Productivity—Demonstrates that given the right working environment, employees can increase their productivity dramatically. You'll learn how to get employees to be involved, energized, more productive and to take ownership. Includes case studies and the latest research on motivation. Stock # 2363XACZ, $17.95/$16.15 AMA Members.

Beyond Customer Satisfaction to Customer Loyalty: The Key to Greater Profitability —Identifies the four stages of a company's evolution toward building customer loyalty and summarizes the key management principles that must guide the transition. Stock # 2362XACZ, $19.95/$17.95 AMA Members.

The New OSHA: A Blueprint for Effective Training and Written Programs— Explains the new law and tells which statutes are most often the subject of investigations and which require training. Models, step-by-step procedures, and additional resources are also included. Stock # 2360XACZ, $24.95/$22.45 AMA Members.

The Management Compass: Steering the Corporation Using Hoshin Planning— Examines the fundamentals of *hoshin planning*, a strategic management methodology which originated in Japan, that is gaining rapid acceptance with U.S. companies. Stock # 2358XACZ, $19.95/$17.95 AMA Members.

Mentoring: Helping Employees Reach Their Full Potential—Shows how mentoring has progressed to an information-age model of helping people learn, offering a wealth of management opportunities for organizational rejuvenation, competitive adaptation, and employee development. Stock # 2357XACZ, $14.95/$13.45 AMA Members.

Complete the **ORDER FORM** on the following page. For faster service, **CALL** , **FAX** , or **E-MAIL** your order.

Visit our web site: www.amanet.org

MANAGEMENT BRIEFING ORDER FORM
(A multiple-copy discount is available. Call for details.)

Please send me the following:

☐ ____ copies of **Recharge Your Team—Keep Them Going and Going...**, Stock # 2366XACZ, $12.95/$11.65 AMA Members.

☐ ____ copies of **The Computer Time Bomb: How to Keep the Century Date Change from Killing Your Organization**, Stock # 2365XACZ, $24.95/$22.45 AMA Members.

☐ ____ copies of **A Better Place to Work: A New Sense of Motivation Leading to Higher Productivity**, Stock # 2363XACZ, $17.95/$16.15 AMA Members.

☐ ____ copies of **Beyond Customer Satisfaction to Customer Loyalty: The Key to Greater Profitability**, Stock # 2362XACZ, $19.95/$17.95 AMA Members.

☐ ____ copies of **The New OSHA: A Blueprint for Effective Training and Written Programs**, Stock # 2360XACZ, $24.95/$22.45 AMA Members.

☐ ____ copies of **The Management Compass: Steering the Corporation Using Hoshin Planning**, Stock # 2358XACZ, $19.95/$17.95 AMA Members.

☐ ____ copies of **Mentoring: Helping Employees Reach Their Full Potential**, Stock # 2357XACZ, $14.95/$13.45 AMA Members.

Name: _____

Title: _____

Organization: _____

Street Address: _____

City, State, Zip: _____

Phone: ( ) _____ Fax: ( ) _____

Applicable sales tax and shipping & handling will be added.

☐ Charge my credit card   ☐ Bill me   ☐ AMA Member

Card # _____ Exp. Date _____

Signature: _____

Purchase Order #: _____

AMA NO-RISK GUARANTEE: If for any reason you are not satisfied, we will credit the purchase price toward another product or refund your money. **No hassles. No loopholes. Just excellent service. That is what AMA is all about.**

**Management Briefings
AMA Publication Services
P.O. Box 319
Saranac Lake, NY 12983
Visit our web site: www.amanet.org**